Materials

Start collecting materials to make the wonderful pictures in this book. You'll need paper and poster board, yarn and felt, sequins and beads, foil, glitter and paints, sponge, and fancy candy wrappers.

You can either make the pictures just the same as the ones in the book, or you can use the ideas to design your own. There are all sorts of exciting and unusual painting techniques for you to try out, too.

Designed by **Jane Warring**
Illustrations by **Lindy Norton**
Pictures made by **Karen Radford**
Photographs by **Peter Millard**

This edition © 1997 Thumbprint Books
Published by Rigby Interactive Library,
an imprint of Rigby Education
a division of Reed Elsevier, Inc.
500 Coventry Lane, Crystal Lake, IL 60014

Printed in Italy

00 99 98 97 96
10 9 8 7 6 5 4 3 2 1

Library of Congress Cataloging-in-Publication Data

King, Penny, 1963-
  Secrets of the sea / Penny King and Clare Roundhill.
    p.   cm. -- (Making pictures)
  Includes index.
  Summary: Gives directions for creating collages featuring the sea
and its inhabitants.
  ISBN 1-57572-193-7 (lib.bdg.)
  1. Collage--Juvenile literature. 2. Sea in art--Juvenile
literature. (1. Collage. 2. Sea in art. 3. Handicraft.)
I. Roundhill, Clare, 1964- . II. Title. III. Series: King,
Penny, 1963- Making pictures.
TT910.K565 1997
702'8'12--DC21

                                                    96-40519
                                                        CIP
                                                         AC

Making Pictures
SECRETS OF THE SEA

Penny King and Clare Roundhill

Contents

A Fancy Sandcastle

Decorate a sandpaper castle with fancy paper shapes, pebbles, and seaweed, and put a bright flag on the top. To make the seaweed glisten, dip strips of green tissue into craft glue. Why not try to decorate the beach, too?

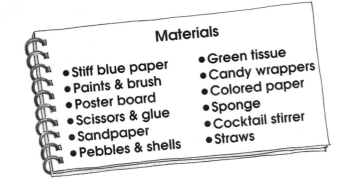

Materials
- Stiff blue paper
- Paints & brush
- Poster board
- Scissors & glue
- Sandpaper
- Pebbles & shells
- Green tissue
- Candy wrappers
- Colored paper
- Sponge
- Cocktail stirrer
- Straws

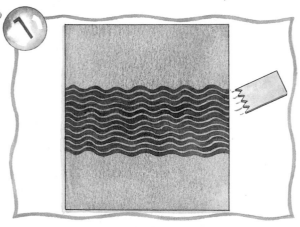

Brush blue paint over the middle of the stiff blue paper. Make wiggly waves (see paint tip).

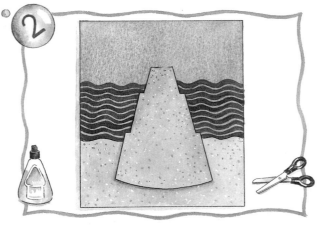

Cut a beach and a sandcastle out of sandpaper. Glue them onto the background paper.

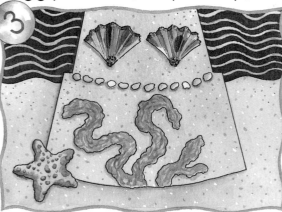

Decorate the castle with candy wrappers cut into fans, tissue seaweed, and tiny pebbles.

Decorate the picture with shells, a bucket, a sponge sun, and starfish. Don't forget a flag!

7

A Lurking Lobster

Let your hands and fingers create the sea creatures in this underwater picture.

You'll need to practice to get perfect lobster, crab, and shrimp prints.

1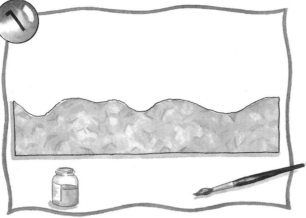

Cut a sea bed from white paper. Brush yellow paint over it. Crumple it. Smooth it out.

2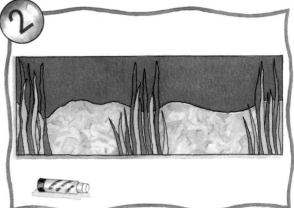

Glue it onto the bottom of the stiff blue paper. Glue on strips of green tissue seaweed.

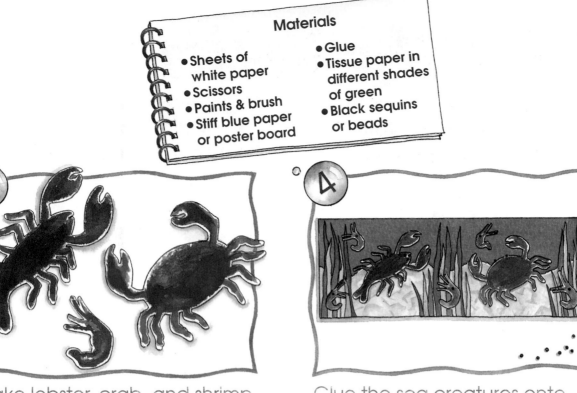

③ Make lobster, crab, and shrimp prints on white paper (see paint tip). Cut them out.

④ Glue the sea creatures onto the sea and sand. Glue on black sequins for their eyes.

PAINT TIP
Cover the side of your little finger with paint. Press it on to white paper to make shrimps. Do the same to print the legs and claws for the lobster and crab. Use the palm of your hand to print the crab's body and the side of your hand for the lobster's body. Make thumb prints for the lobster's tail.

9

A Terrific Turtle

Use any colors you want to make this shiny turtle. Trace the yogurt container onto the background paper to see where to position his head, legs, and tail. Tape the fish onto pipe cleaners and stick them all over the sea.

Materials

- Empty plastic yogurt container
- Thick, shiny paper
- Scissors & glue
- Stiff green paper
- Glitter
- Shiny poster board
- Red sequins
- Tissue paper
- Pipe cleaners
- Tape

Cut the shiny paper into little squares. Glue them in rows to the outside of the container.

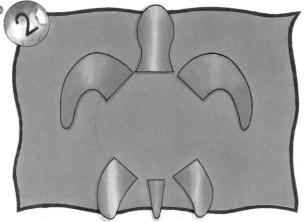

Cut out the turtle's head, legs, and tail from shiny poster board. Glue them onto green paper.

Glue the container in position for the turtle's body. Decorate it with glitter. Add sequin eyes.

Make paper fish with tissue fins and tails. Tape them onto pipe cleaners and then to the sea.

PAINT TIP
Instead of using shiny paper,
you can paint the fishes'
bodies. Draw them on plain
paper and paint them bright
colors with pretty patterns.
Cut them out and add tissue
fins and tails.

11

Jolly Jellyfish

Make these jolly jellyfish floating in the deep, dark sea. Use shiny silver foil for their bodies and lots of glittery, colored pipe cleaners for their tentacles.

1

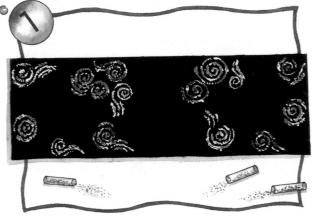

Cut a long piece of stiff black paper. Dab swirls of glue over it and cover them with glitter.

2

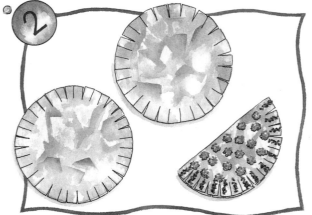

Draw and cut out circles of foil. Snip the edges. Fold them in half. Add glitter.

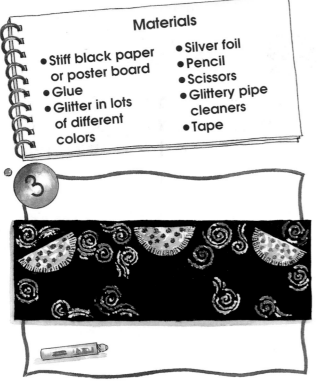

Materials

- Stiff black paper or poster board
- Glue
- Glitter in lots of different colors
- Silver foil
- Pencil
- Scissors
- Glittery pipe cleaners
- Tape

PAINT TIP
Instead of using black poster board, paint your own background. Brush thick black paint over white paper. Let it dry.

Dab glue on the back of each folded circle. Glue them onto the background paper.

Tape glittery pipe cleaners on the inside of each jellyfish. Fold them in half again.

13

A Fabulous Mermaid

Make a picture of a pretty mermaid from poster board or felt. Give her yarn hair, a sparkly tail, and a smiling face. Make her jewels out of shiny paper and tiny beads. Then put her in the deep, swirly sea with lots of colorful seahorses.

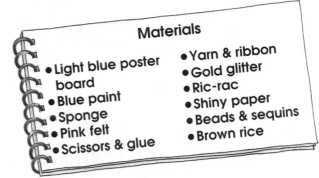

Materials

- Light blue poster board
- Blue paint
- Sponge
- Pink felt
- Scissors & glue
- Yarn & ribbon
- Gold glitter
- Ric-rac
- Shiny paper
- Beads & sequins
- Brown rice

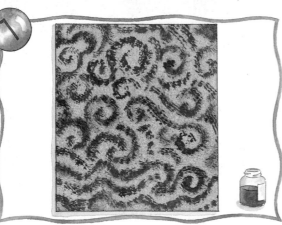

Sponge a dark blue sea on top of the light blue poster board (see paint tip). Let it dry.

Draw a mermaid on pink felt and cut her out. Glue her to the middle of the sea.

Decorate the mermaid with a glitter and ric-rac tail, yarn hair, a bow, and shiny jewels.

Glue cut-out board seahorses on the sea. Glue on a brown rice and gold glitter sea bed.

PAINT TIP
Put dark blue paint in
an old plate. Dip a small
sponge into the paint.
Dab it in swirls over the
light blue background
to give the effect of
big frothy waves.

Paddling Toes

This silly picture of feet paddling in the sea will make people laugh.

Use dried beans for the pebbles and tissue paper for the feet and legs.

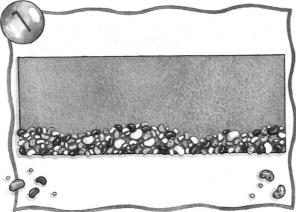

Cover the bottom of the stiff blue paper with glue and place dried beans on it.

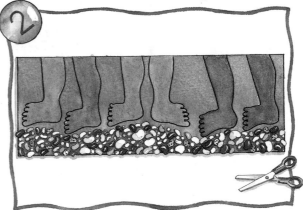

Cut three pairs of tissue legs and feet. Glue them down so they are standing on the beans.

PAINT TIP
Cut a fish shape out of a sponge. Pour some paint into a plate. Dip the sponge fish in the paint and print it onto the picture. It is best to practice first on a sheet of paper before you print onto your picture. You may need to use slightly thicker or watery paint.

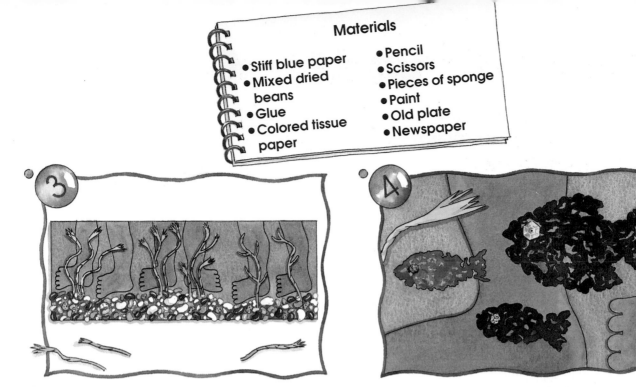

Cut little strips of green tissue and twist them into seaweed. Glue them onto the sea bed.

Make a sponge fish (see paint tip). Print fish in lots of different colors on the sea and legs.

17

An Underwater Garden

Use an old shoebox or a cardboard box to make this underwater garden. Fill it with colorful fish, a seahorse, lots of pretty shells, and some wiggly seaweed. You can also add a chest overflowing with sparkling treasures.

Materials
- Shoebox
- Paints & brush
- Shiny green paper
- Scissors & glue
- Shells
- Small pebbles or sand
- Poster board
- Sequins or beads
- Needle & thread
- Tape

Paint the box blue (see paint tip). Cut out paper seaweed shapes. Glue them to the box.

Spread the bottom of the box with glue. Place small pebbles or sand and shells all over it.

Cut fish out of poster board. Paint them with spots or stripes. Glue on sequins or bead eyes.

Thread cotton through each fish. Knot it. Hang the fish with tape from the top of the box.

A Rippling Rockpool

Cut a rockpool shape from blue paper. Cut a smaller white one the same shape.

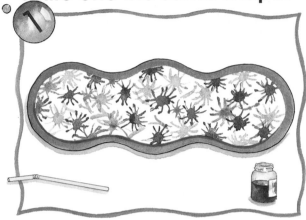

Blow blobs of paint over the white paper (see paint tip). Glue it onto the blue paper.

Fill the pool with leafy fish and ripples, with a fringe of crêpe paper seaweed.

Cut four strips of blue and green crêpe paper. Cut a fringe along each one, like this.

PAINT TIP
Before you start, cover your work surface with newspaper as this project can be messy. Put drops of watery blue paint onto white paper. Gently blow the drops through a straw to make the paint spread in all directions. Instead of using only one color, try blowing several different colors, one on top of the other.

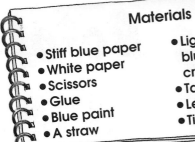

Materials

- Stiff blue paper
- White paper
- Scissors
- Glue
- Blue paint
- A straw
- Light and dark blue and green crêpe paper
- Tape
- Leaves
- Tiny beads

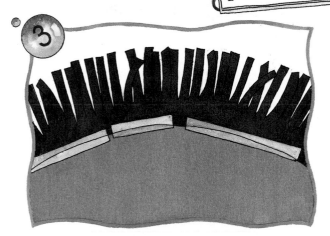

Tape the crêpe strips, one on top of the other, to the back of the blue paper. Fluff them out.

Cut big and small fish shapes out of leaves. Stick them onto the rockpool. Add beady eyes.

21

A Grasping Octopus

Look at how much treasure this lucky octopus has in its eight long arms! Paint your own octopus floating in a blue sea. Give it treasure galore, made with shiny materials you can find around the house. Put a gold crown on its head.

Materials
- Blue & green poster board
- Pencil
- Scissors & glue
- Sequins
- Red yarn
- Green paint
- Old plate
- Pipe cleaners
- Tissue paper
- Silver foil
- Shiny paper

1 Draw an octopus on green board. Glue on beady eyes and a yarn mouth. Cut it out.

2 Fingerpaint green suckers on the arms (see paint tip). Glue the octopus on the blue board.

3 Twist two pipe cleaners into a ring. Make a necklace of tissue balls. Make a goblet out of foil.

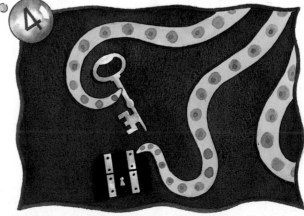

4 Cut other treasures from shiny paper. Glue one on the end of each tentacle.

23

Fish in a Net

Save lots of colorful candy wrappers and shiny paper to make flashy fish for a picture like this. Put some of the fish in a net with bobbing cork buoys and string. Cover the bottom of the sea with seaweed and lurking sea creatures.

Materials

- White board
- White candle
- Paints & brush
- Shiny paper
- Pencil
- Scissors & glue
- Sequins
- Onion bag
- String
- Cork circles
- Colored paper
- Tissue paper

Make waxy waves on the white poster board and cover them with blue paint (see paint tip).

Draw fish on shiny paper. Cut them out. Decorate them with paper shapes and sequin eyes.

Glue fish in the net and on the sea. Thread string through the net. Glue cork circles on top.

Cut out tissue seaweed and paper sea creatures. Glue them onto the bottom of the sea.

24

PAINT TIP
Draw wavy lines all over the poster board with the thick end of a candle. Brush watery blue paint over the paper. The wax lines will show through the paint.

25

A Whale of a Time

Have fun blowing bubbles to make a frothy sea for these whales to swim in.

Cut out a frilly border of green seaweed to frame your underwater picture.

In a large bowl, mix some blue paint, a squirt of dish soap, and a little water.

Put a straw into the mixture. Blow hard until bubbles puff up above the rim of the bowl.

PAINT TIP
To make clean bubble prints, lay the paper gently on top of the bubbles. Be careful not to press the paper down onto the rim of the bowl. After each print, blow the mixture again to make more bubbles. If your paint mixture is not bubbly enough, add a little more dish soap.

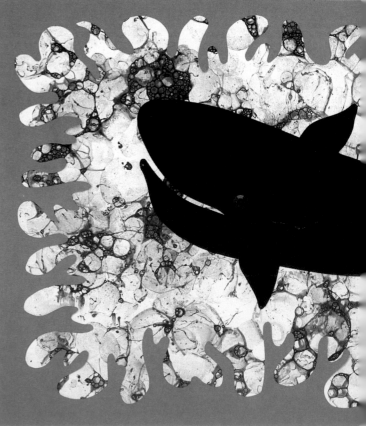

Materials

- Mixing bowl
- Blue paint
- Dish soap
- Pitcher of water
- Spoon
- A straw
- White, black, & green paper
- Scissors
- Glue
- Sequins

③

To make a foamy sea, cover a long sheet of white paper with bubble prints (see paint tip).

④

Glue on two paper whales. Glue on sequin eyes. Cut out and glue on a green paper border.

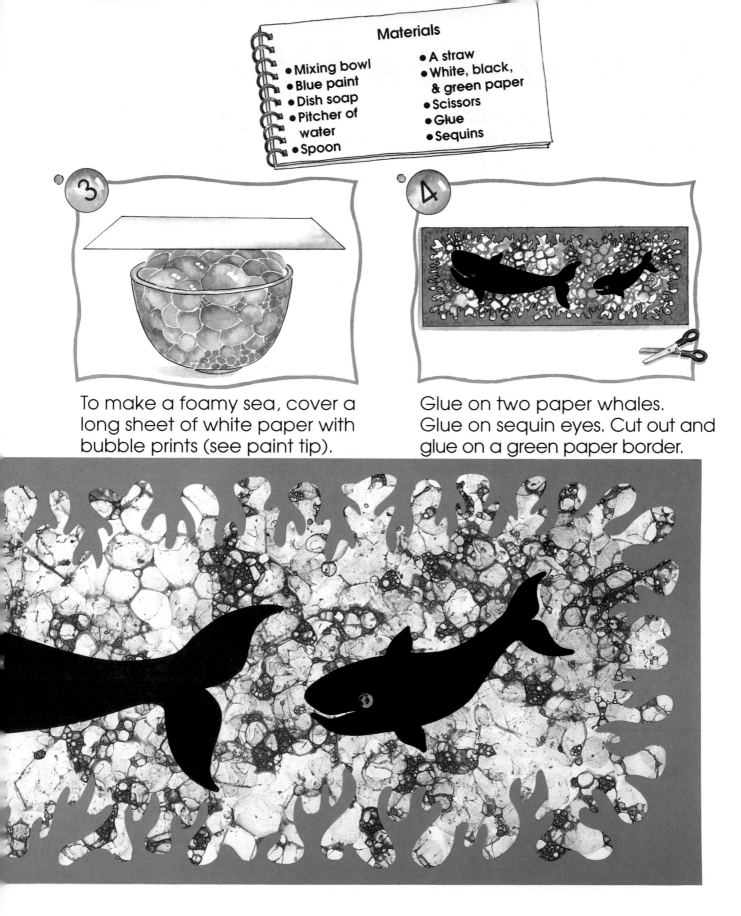

27

Sparkling Starfish

Create an unusual picture of colorful felt starfish washed up on a beach made of lentils, beans, and barley. To make the starfish sparkle and glisten, cover them with pearly beads and sequins. Print a fishy border with potato stamps.

Materials

- Yellow & green poster board
- Craft glue
- Dried lentils, beans, & barley
- Scissors
- Felt in different bright colors
- Beads & sequins
- Big potato
- Dish & knife
- Paints & brush

Spread glue over the yellow poster board. Cover it with lentils, beans, and barley.

Cut out two big and two little starfish shapes from different colored felt.

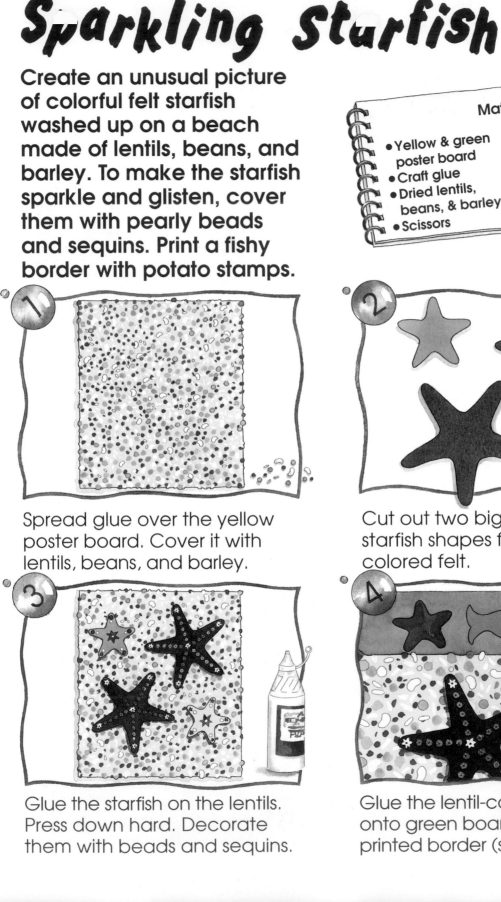

Glue the starfish on the lentils. Press down hard. Decorate them with beads and sequins.

Glue the lentil-covered board onto green board. Make a printed border (see paint tip).

PAINT TIP
Cut a big potato in half.
Ask an adult to help you cut
a fish shape out of each
half. Put paint in a dish and
press the potato stamp
into it. Print them onto
green poster board.

29